40

HADITH

on Knowledge

Introduction

In the name of Allah, the Most Gracious, the Most Merciful.

Praise be to Allah, the Sustainer of all existence, the Bestower of knowledge and wisdom. Peace and blessings be upon the noble Messenger, Muhammad (Sallallahu alaihi wasallam), the beacon of divine guidance and the source of profound wisdom that continues to illuminate the hearts and minds of believers throughout the ages.

It is with great joy and humility that we present to you "**40 Hadith on Knowledge**," a sacred compilation that delves into the essence of seeking knowledge in Islam. Within these pages lie the timeless sayings of the Prophet (Sallallahu alaihi wasallam), each a radiant gem of wisdom, shedding light on the significance of knowledge as a path to spiritual growth and enlightenment.

In a world brimming with information, the pursuit of true knowledge, infused with divine wisdom, becomes paramount. As believers, we are entrusted with the sacred duty of seeking understanding, discovering truth, and sharing knowledge for the betterment of ourselves and humanity at large.

Through the profound teachings of the Prophet (Sallallahu alaihi wasallam), we are reminded that knowledge is not simply a means to acquire facts, but a key to unlock the gates of closeness to our Creator. Each Hadith within this book unveils a treasure trove of insights, guiding us towards intellectual curiosity, humility, and the application of knowledge for the betterment of society.

Let us delve into these sacred sayings with open hearts and receptive souls, for it is in the pursuit of knowledge that we find the means to navigate the challenges of life, deepen our understanding of the Divine, and live a purposeful and righteous existence.

As you embark on this journey, may your soul be nourished with the timeless wisdom of the Prophet (Sallallahu alaihi wasallam), and may the pursuit of knowledge become a means of drawing closer to Allah, seeking His pleasure, and finding solace in His infinite wisdom.

May "**40 Hadith on Knowledge**" serve as a source of inspiration, enlightenment, and transformative growth, igniting the flame of curiosity within you and fostering a deep sense of reverence for the pursuit of knowledge in Islam.

In the spirit of seeking knowledge, let us embark on this journey together, humbly seeking Allah's guidance and blessings, for He is the Bestower of knowledge, and to Him, we turn in all matters.

Peace and blessings be upon the Prophet Muhammad (Sallallahu alaihi wasallam) and upon all who seek knowledge in His blessed name.

Aicha Mhamed

Hadith 1

Anas ibn Malik reported: The Messenger of Allah, peace and blessings be upon him, said:

طَلَبُ الْعِلْمِ فَرِيضَةٌ عَلَى كُلِّ مُسْلِمٍ

Seeking knowledge is an obligation upon every Muslim.

Hadith 2

Abu Huraira reported: The Messenger of Allah, peace and blessings be upon him, said:

وَمَنْ سَلَكَ طَرِيقًا يَلْتَمِسُ فِيهِ عِلْمًا سَهَّلَ اللَّهُ لَهُ بِهِ طَرِيقًا إِلَى الْجَنَّةِ وَمَا اجْتَمَعَ قَوْمٌ فِي بَيْتٍ مِنْ بُيُوتِ اللَّهِ يَتْلُونَ كِتَابَ اللَّهِ وَيَتَدَارَسُونَهُ بَيْنَهُمْ إِلاَّ نَزَلَتْ عَلَيْهِمُ السَّكِينَةُ وَغَشِيَتْهُمُ الرَّحْمَةُ وَحَفَّتْهُمُ الْمَلاَئِكَةُ وَذَكَرَهُمُ اللَّهُ فِيمَنْ عِنْدَهُ

Whoever travels a path in search of knowledge, Allah will make easy for him a path to Paradise. People do not gather in the houses of Allah, reciting the book of Allah and studying it together, but that tranquility will descend upon them, mercy will cover them, angels will surround them, and Allah will mention them to those near him.

Hadith 3

Abu Darda reported: The Messenger of Allah, peace and blessings be upon him, said:

وَإِنَّ الْمَلَائِكَةَ لَتَضَعُ أَجْنِحَتَهَا رِضًا لِطَالِبِ الْعِلْمِ وَإِنَّ الْعَالِمَ لَيَسْتَغْفِرُ لَهُ مَنْ فِي السَّمَوَاتِ وَمَنْ فِي الْأَرْضِ وَالْحِيتَانُ فِي جَوْفِ الْمَاءِ وَإِنَّ فَضْلَ الْعَالِمِ عَلَى الْعَابِدِ كَفَضْلِ الْقَمَرِ لَيْلَةَ الْبَدْرِ عَلَى سَائِرِ الْكَوَاكِبِ وَإِنَّ الْعُلَمَاءَ وَرَثَةُ الْأَنْبِيَاءِ وَإِنَّ الْأَنْبِيَاءَ لَمْ يُوَرِّثُوا دِينَارًا وَلَا دِرْهَمًا وَرَّثُوا الْعِلْمَ فَمَنْ أَخَذَهُ أَخَذَ بِحَظٍّ وَافِرٍ

Verily, the angels lower their wings for the seeker of knowledge. The inhabitants of the heavens and earth, even the fish in the depths of the water, seek forgiveness for the scholar. The virtue of the scholar over the worshiper is like the superiority of the moon over the stars. The scholars are the inheritors of the Prophets. They do not leave behind gold or silver coins, but rather they leave behind knowledge. Whoever has taken hold of it has been given an abundant share.

Hadith 4

Abu Umamah reported: The Messenger of Allah, peace and blessings be upon him, said:

فَضْلُ الْعَالِمِ عَلَى الْعَابِدِ كَفَضْلِي عَلَى أَدْنَاكُمْ إِنَّ اللَّهَ وَمَلَائِكَتَهُ وَأَهْلَ السَّمَوَاتِ وَالْأَرَضِينَ حَتَّى النَّمْلَةَ فِي جُحْرِهَا وَحَتَّى الْحُوتَ لَيُصَلُّونَ عَلَى مُعَلِّمِ النَّاسِ الْخَيْرَ

The virtue of the scholar over the worshiper is like my virtue over the least of you. Verily, Allah, his angels, the inhabitants of the heavens and earth, even the ant in his hole and the fish, send blessings upon the one who teaches people what is good.

Fudayl ibn 'Iyad, may Allah have mercy on him, said:

عَالِمٌ عَامِلٌ مُعَلِّمٌ يُدْعَى كَبِيرًا فِي مَلَكُوتِ السَّمَوَاتِ

A scholar who works in teaching has a high status in the domain of the heavens.

Hadith 5

Mu'awiyah reported: The Messenger of Allah, peace and blessings be upon him, said:

مَنْ يُرِدْ اللَّهُ بِهِ خَيْرًا يُفَقِّهْهُ فِي الدِّينِ

If Allah intends goodness for someone, he gives him understanding of the religion.

In another narration, the Prophet said:

يَا أَيُّهَا النَّاسُ إِنَّمَا الْعِلْمُ بِالتَّعَلُّمِ وَالْفِقْهُ بِالتَّفَقُّهِ وَمَنْ يُرِدِ اللَّهُ بِهِ خَيْرًا يُفَقِّهْهُ فِي الدِّينِ وَإِنَّمَا يَخْشَى اللَّهَ مِنْ عِبَادِهِ الْعُلَمَاءُ

O people, knowledge only comes by learning and understanding only comes by seeking understanding. For whomever Allah intends good, he gives him understanding of the religion. Verily, only those with knowledge fear Allah among his servants.

The Quran (35:28)

Hadith 6

Abu Huraira reported: The Messenger of Allah, peace and blessings be upon him, said:

خَيْرُكُمْ إِسْلَامًا أَحَاسِنُكُمْ أَخْلَاقًا إِذَا فَقُهُوا

The best of you in Islam are those with the best character, if they have religious understanding.

Malik ibn Anas, may Allah have mercy on him, said:

إِنَّ حَقًّا عَلَى مَنْ طَلَبَ الْعِلْمَ أَنْ يَكُونَ لَهُ وَقَارٌ وَسَكِينَةٌ وَخَشْيَةٌ وَأَنْ يَكُونَ مُتَّبِعًا لِآثَارِ مَنْ مَضَى قَبْلَهُ

Verily, it is the duty of a student of knowledge to behave with dignity, tranquility, and reverence, and to follow the way of those who came before him.

Hadith 7

Abu Musa reported: The Prophet, peace and blessings be upon him, said:

إِنَّ مَثَلَ مَا بَعَثَنِيَ اللهُ بِهِ عَزَّ وَجَلَّ مِنَ الْهُدَى وَالْعِلْمِ كَمَثَلِ غَيْثٍ أَصَابَ أَرْضًا فَكَانَتْ مِنْهَا طَائِفَةٌ طَيِّبَةٌ قَبِلَتِ الْمَاءَ فَأَنْبَتَتِ الْكَلَأَ وَالْعُشْبَ الْكَثِيرَ وَكَانَ مِنْهَا أَجَادِبُ أَمْسَكَتِ الْمَاءَ فَنَفَعَ اللهُ بِهَا النَّاسَ فَشَرِبُوا مِنْهَا وَسَقَوْا وَرَعَوْا وَأَصَابَ طَائِفَةً مِنْهَا أُخْرَى إِنَّمَا هِيَ قِيعَانٌ لَا تُمْسِكُ مَاءً وَلَا تُنْبِتُ كَلَأً فَذَلِكَ مَثَلُ مَنْ فَقُهَ فِي دِينِ اللهِ وَنَفَعَهُ بِمَا بَعَثَنِيَ اللهُ بِهِ فَعَلِمَ وَعَلَّمَ وَمَثَلُ مَنْ لَمْ يَرْفَعْ بِذَلِكَ رَأْسًا وَلَمْ يَقْبَلْ هُدَى اللهِ الَّذِي أُرْسِلْتُ بِهِ

Verily, the parable of the guidance and knowledge that Allah Almighty sent with me is the likeness of rain falling upon the earth. Among them is a good group which receives the water and thus there is abundant growth of herbage and grass. Among them is a barren land which retains the water and thus Allah benefits people from it; they drink from it and graze their animals. And it falls upon another group which is only abysmal; it does not retain water, nor does herbage grow.

Such is the parable of one who understands the religion of Allah and benefits from what Allah sent with me; he learns and he teaches. Such is the parable of one who does not raise his head and does not accept the guidance Allah sent with me.

Hadith 8

Abdullah ibn Mas'ud reported: The Prophet, peace and blessings be upon him, said:

لَا حَسَدَ إِلَّا فِي اثْنَتَيْنِ رَجُلٌ آتَاهُ اللهُ مَالًا فَسُلِّطَ عَلَى هَلَكَتِهِ فِي الْحَقّ وَرَجُلٌ آتَاهُ اللهُ الْحِكْمَةَ فَهُوَ يَقْضِي بِهَا وَيُعَلِّمُهَا

There is no envy but in two cases: a man whom Allah has given wealth and he spends it rightly, and a man whom Allah has given wisdom and he judges and teaches with it.

Hadith 9

Uthman bin Affan reported: The Prophet, peace and blessings be upon him, said:

خَيْرُكُمْ مَنْ تَعَلَّمَ الْقُرْآنَ وَعَلَّمَهُ

The best of you are those who learn the Quran and teach it.

Hadith 10

Sahl ibn Sa'd reported: The Prophet, peace and blessings be upon him, said:

وَاللَّهِ لَأَنْ يَهْدِيَ اللَّهُ بِكَ رَجُلًا خَيْرٌ لَكَ مِنْ أَنْ يَكُونَ لَكَ حُمْرُ النَّعَمِ

By Allah, that Allah guides a man through you is better for you than a herd of expensive red camels.

Hadith 11

Abdullah ibn Amr reported: The Prophet, peace and blessings be upon him, said:

بَلِّغُوا عَنِّي وَلَوْ آيَةً وَحَدِّثُوا عَنْ بَنِي إِسْرَائِيلَ وَلَا حَرَجَ وَمَنْ كَذَبَ عَلَيَّ مُتَعَمِّدًا فَلْيَتَبَوَّأْ مَقْعَدَهُ مِنْ النَّارِ

Convey from me, even a single verse. Narrate from the children of Israel, for there is no blame in it. Whoever deliberately lies about me, let him take his seat in Hellfire.

Abdullah ibn Amr reported:

كَانَ نَبِيُّ اللهِ صَلَّى اللهُ عَلَيْهِ وَسَلَّمَ يُحَدِّثُنَا عَنْ بَنِي إِسْرَائِيلَ حَتَّى يُصْبِح مَا يَقُومُ إِلَّا إِلَى عُظْمِ صَلَاةٍ

The Prophet, peace and blessings be upon him, would narrate stories from the children of Israel until the morning came. The Prophet would not stand but for the greatness of prayer.

Al-Shafi'i, may Allah have mercy on him, said:

مِنَ الْمَعْلُومِ أَنَّ النَّبِيَّ صَلَّى اللهُ عَلَيْهِ وَسَلَّمَ لَا يُجِيزُ التَّحَدُّثَ بِالْكَذِبِ فَالْمَعْنَى حَدِّثُوا عَنْ بَنِي إِسْرَائِيلَ بِمَا لَا تَعْلَمُونَ كَذِبَهُ

It is known that the Prophet (s) did not approve of falsehood. Thus, the meaning is to narrate from the children of Israel what is known not to be false.

Hadith 13

Zayd ibn Thabit reported: The Messenger of Allah, peace and blessings be upon him, said:

نَضَّرَ اللَّهُ امْرَأً سَمِعَ مِنَّا حَدِيثًا فَحَفِظَهُ حَتَّى يُبَلِّغَهُ فَرُبَّ حَامِلِ فِقْهٍ إِلَى مَنْ هُوَ أَفْقَهُ مِنْهُ وَرُبَّ حَامِلِ فِقْهٍ لَيْسَ بِفَقِيهٍ

May Allah brighten the face of a person who hears a tradition from us and he memorizes it until he can convey it to others. Perhaps he will convey it to one who understands better than him, and perhaps one who conveys knowledge does not understand it himself.

Hadith 14

Abu Huraira reported: The Messenger of Allah, peace and blessings be upon him, said:

مَنْ دَعَا إِلَى هُدًى كَانَ لَهُ مِنَ الْأَجْرِ مِثْلُ أُجُورِ مَنْ تَبِعَهُ لاَ يَنْقُصُ ذَلِكَ مِنْ أُجُورِهِمْ شَيْئًا وَمَنْ دَعَا إِلَى ضَلَالَةٍ كَانَ عَلَيْهِ مِنَ الإِثْمِ مِثْلُ آثَامِ مَنْ تَبِعَهُ لاَ يَنْقُصُ ذَلِكَ مِنْ آثَامِهِمْ شَيْئًا

Whoever calls to guidance will have a reward similar to those who follow him, without detracting from their rewards at all. Whoever calls to misguidance will have sin upon him similar to those who follow him, without detracting from their sins at all.

Hadith 15

'Amr ibn 'Awf reported: The Messenger of Allah, peace and blessings be upon him, said:

اعْلَمْ إِنَّهُ مَنْ أَحْيَا سُنَّةً مِنْ سُنَّتِي قَدْ أُمِيتَتْ بَعْدِي فَإِنَّ لَهُ مِنْ الْأَجْرِ مِثْلَ
مَنْ عَمِلَ بِهَا مِنْ غَيْرِ أَنْ يَنْقُصَ مِنْ أُجُورِهِمْ شَيْئًا وَمَنْ ابْتَدَعَ بِدْعَةَ
ضَلَالَةٍ لَا تُرْضِي اللَّهَ وَرَسُولَهُ كَانَ عَلَيْهِ مِثْلُ آثَامِ مَنْ عَمِلَ بِهَا لَا
يَنْقُصُ ذَلِكَ مِنْ أَوْزَارِ النَّاسِ شَيْئًا

Know that whoever revives a tradition from my Sunnah if it has died out after me, he will have a reward like those who act upon it without diminishing any of their rewards. Whoever innovates a misguided heresy not pleasing to Allah and his messenger, he will have a sin like those who act upon it without diminishing any of the people's burdens.

Hadith 16

Abu Huraira reported: The Messenger of Allah, peace and blessings be upon him, said:

إِذَا مَاتَ الْإِنْسَانُ انْقَطَعَ عَنْهُ عَمَلُهُ إِلَّا مِنْ ثَلَاثَةٍ إِلَّا مِنْ صَدَقَةٍ جَارِيَةٍ
أَوْ عِلْمٍ يُنْتَفَعُ بِهِ أَوْ وَلَدٍ صَالِحٍ يَدْعُو لَهُ

When the human being dies, his deeds end except for three: ongoing charity, beneficial knowledge, or a righteous child who prays for him.

In another narration, the Prophet said:

إِنَّ مِمَّا يَلْحَقُ الْمُؤْمِنَ مِنْ عَمَلِهِ وَحَسَنَاتِهِ بَعْدَ مَوْتِهِ عِلْمًا عَلَّمَهُ وَنَشَرَهُ
وَوَلَدًا صَالِحًا تَرَكَهُ وَمُصْحَفًا وَرَّثَهُ أَوْ مَسْجِدًا بَنَاهُ أَوْ بَيْتًا لِابْنِ السَّبِيلِ
بَنَاهُ أَوْ نَهْرًا أَجْرَاهُ أَوْ صَدَقَةً أَخْرَجَهَا مِنْ مَالِهِ فِي صِحَّتِهِ وَحَيَاتِهِ
يَلْحَقُهُ مِنْ بَعْدِ مَوْتِهِ

Hadith 16

Verily, among the good deeds that will join a believer after his death are these: knowledge which he taught and spread, a righteous child he leaves behind, a copy of the Quran he leaves for inheritance, a mosque he has built, a house he built for travelers, a well he has dug, and charity distributed from his wealth while he was alive and well. These deeds will join him after his death.

Hadith 17

Anas ibn Malik reported: The Messenger of Allah, peace and blessings be upon him, said:

مَنْ خَرَجَ فِي طَلَبِ الْعِلْمِ كَانَ فِي سَبِيلِ اللَّهِ حَتَّى يَرْجِعَ

Whoever goes out seeking knowledge is in the way of Allah until he returns.

Hadith 18

Abu Sa'id al-Khudri reported: The Messenger of Allah, peace and blessings be upon him, said:

لَنْ يَشْبَعَ الْمُؤْمِنُ مِنْ خَيْرٍ يَسْمَعُهُ حَتَّى يَكُونَ مُنْتَهَاهُ الْجَنَّةُ

The believer is never satisfied from learning good until he arrives in Paradise.

Malik ibn Anas, may Allah have mercy on him, said:

لا يَنْبَغِي لِأَحَدٍ يَكُونُ عِنْدَهُ الْعِلْمُ أَنْ يَتْرُكَ التَّعَلُّمَ

It is not befitting for anyone with knowledge to give up learning.

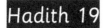

Abu Huraira reported: The Messenger of Allah, peace and blessings be upon him, said:

أَلَا إِنَّ الدُّنْيَا مَلْعُونَةٌ مَلْعُونٌ مَا فِيهَا إِلَّا ذِكْرُ اللَّهِ وَمَا وَالاهُ وَعَالِمٌ أَوْ مُتَعَلِّمٌ

Is not the world cursed and everything in it? Except for the remembrance of Allah and what facilitates it, the scholar or the student.

Abdullah ibn Amr reported: The Messenger of Allah, peace and blessings be upon him, said:

إِنَّ اللَّهَ لَا يَقْبِضُ الْعِلْمَ انْتِزَاعًا يَنْتَزِعُهُ مِنْ الْعِبَادِ وَلَكِنْ يَقْبِضُ الْعِلْمَ بِقَبْضِ الْعُلَمَاءِ حَتَّى إِذَا لَمْ يُبْقِ عَالِمًا اتَّخَذَ النَّاسُ رُءُوسًا جُهَّالًا فَسُئِلُوا فَأَفْتَوْا بِغَيْرِ عِلْمٍ فَضَلُّوا وَأَضَلُّوا

Verily, Allah does not withhold knowledge by snatching it away from his servants, but rather he withholds knowledge by taking the souls scholars, until no scholar remains and people follow ignorant leaders. They are asked and they issue judgments without knowledge. Thus, they are astray and lead others astray.

Hadith 21

Abu Huraira reported: The Messenger of Allah, peace and blessings be upon him, said:

مَنْ دَخَلَ مَسْجِدَنَا هَذَا لِيَتَعَلَّمَ خَيْرًا أَوْ لِيُعَلِّمَهُ كَانَ كَالْمُجَاهِدِ فِي سَبِيلِ اللهِ وَمَنْ دَخَلَهُ لِغَيْرِ ذَلِكَ كَانَ كَالنَّاظِرِ إِلَى مَا لَيْسَ لَهُ

Whoever enters our mosque in order to teach goodness, or to learn it himself, he is striving in jihad in the way of Allah. Whoever enters it for another reason, he is viewing what does not belong to him.

Abu Bakr ibn Abdur Rahman, may Allah have mercy on him, said:

مَنْ غَدَا أَوْ رَاحَ إِلَى الْمَسْجِدِ لَا يُرِيدُ غَيْرَهُ لِيَتَعَلَّمَ خَيْرًا أَوْ لِيُعَلِّمَهُ ثُمَّ رَجَعَ إِلَى بَيْتِهِ كَانَ كَالْمُجَاهِدِ فِي سَبِيلِ اللهِ رَجَعَ غَانِمًا

Whoever departs to the mosque in the morning, intending to go nowhere else and to teach goodness, or to learn it himself, and then he returns to his house, he is like one who strives in jihad in the way of Allah and returns with spoils.

Hadith 22

Abdullah ibn Mas'ud reported: The Messenger of Allah, peace and blessings be upon him, said:

مَنْهُومَانِ لا يَشْبَعَانِ طَالِبُهُمَا طَالِبُ عِلْمٍ وَطَالِبُ الدُّنْيَا

The seekers of two concerns are never satisfied: the seeker of knowledge and the seeker of the world.

Hadith 23

Abu Huraira reported: The Messenger of Allah, peace and blessings be upon him, said:

قَالَ موسى فَأَيُّ عِبَادِكَ أَعْلَمُ قَالَ الله عَالِمٌ لا يَشْبَعُ مِنَ الْعِلْمِ يَجْمَعُ عِلْمَ النَّاسِ إِلَى عِلْمِهِ

Moses said: Who are the most knowledgeable of your servants? Allah said: A scholar who is unsatisfied with his knowledge and adds the knowledge of people to his own.

Hadith 24

Safwan ibn 'Assal reported: The Prophet, peace and blessings be upon him, said:

مَا مِنْ خَارِجٍ خَرَجَ مِنْ بَيْتِهِ فِي طَلَبِ الْعِلْمِ إِلَّا وَضَعَتْ لَهُ الْمَلَائِكَةُ أَجْنِحَتَهَا رِضًا بِمَا يَصْنَعُ

No one leaves their house in search of knowledge but that angels will lower their wings in approval of what he is doing.

Hadith 25

Ka'b ibn Malik reported: The Prophet, peace and blessings be upon him, said:

مَنْ طَلَبَ الْعِلْمَ لِيُجَارِيَ بِهِ الْعُلَمَاءَ أَوْ لِيُمَارِيَ بِهِ السُّفَهَاءَ أَوْ يَصْرِفَ بِهِ وُجُوهَ النَّاسِ إِلَيْهِ أَدْخَلَهُ اللَّهُ النَّارَ

Whoever seeks knowledge to impress the scholars, to argue with the foolish, or to attract the attention of people, Allah will admit him into Hellfire.

Hadith 26

Abu Huraira reported: The Messenger of Allah, peace and blessings be upon him, said:

مَنْ تَعَلَّمَ عِلْمًا مِمَّا يُبْتَغَى بِهِ وَجْهُ اللهِ عَزَّ وَجَلَّ لَا يَتَعَلَّمُهُ إِلَّا لِيُصِيبَ بِهِ
عَرَضًا مِنْ الدُّنْيَا لَمْ يَجِدْ عَرْفَ الْجَنَّةِ يَوْمَ الْقِيَامَةِ

Whoever seeks knowledge that should be sought for the sake of Allah Almighty, but only to gain some worldly benefit, he will never know the fragrance Paradise on the Day of Resurrection.

Hadith 27

Abu Huraira reported: The Messenger of Allah, peace and blessings be upon him, said:

مَنْ سُئِلَ عَنْ عِلْمٍ عَلِمَهُ ثُمَّ كَتَمَهُ أُلْجِمَ يَوْمَ الْقِيَامَةِ بِلِجَامٍ مِنْ نَارٍ

Whoever is asked for knowledge and he conceals it, Allah will clothe him with a bridle of fire on the Day of Resurrection.

Hadith 28

Jabir reported: The Messenger of Allah, peace and blessings be upon him, said:

سَلُوا اللَّهَ عِلْمًا نَافِعًا وَتَعَوَّذُوا بِاللَّهِ مِنْ عِلْمٍ لَا يَنْفَعُ

Ask Allah for beneficial knowledge and seek refuge in Allah from knowledge without benefit.

Hadith 29

Ibn Abbas reported: The Messenger of Allah, peace and blessings be upon him, said:

مَنْ قَالَ فِي الْقُرْآنِ بِغَيْرِ عِلْمٍ فَلْيَتَبَوَّأْ مَقْعَدَهُ مِنَ النَّارِ

Whoever speaks on the Quran without knowledge, let him take his seat in Hellfire.

Hadith 30

Ibn Umar reported: The Messenger of Allah, peace and blessings be upon him, said:

إِنَّ اللَّهَ لَا يَجْمَعُ أُمَّتِي عَلَى ضَلَالَةٍ وَيَدُ اللَّهِ مَعَ الْجَمَاعَةِ

Verily, Allah will not let my nation agree upon misguidance. The hand of Allah is over the united community.

Al-Tirmidhi commented on this tradition, saying:

الْجَمَاعَةِ عِنْدَ أَهْلِ الْعِلْمِ هُمْ أَهْلُ الْفِقْهِ وَالْعِلْمِ وَالْحَدِيثِ

The interpretation of the united community, according to the scholars, are the people of Fiqh, knowledge, and Hadith.

Hadith 31

Sa'd ibn Abi Waqqas reported: The Messenger of Allah, peace and blessings be upon him, said:

فَضْلُ الْعِلْمِ أَحَبُّ إِلَيَّ مِنْ فَضْلِ الْعِبَادَةِ وَخَيْرُ دِينِكُمُ الْوَرَعُ

The virtue of knowledge is more beloved to me than the virtue of worship, and the best of your religion is piety.

Hadith 32

Ziyad ibn Labid reported: The Prophet, peace and blessings be upon him, said:

ذَاكَ عِنْدَ أَوَانِ ذَهَابِ الْعِلْمِ

There will be a time when knowledge disappears.

Ziyad said, "O Messenger of Allah, how can knowledge disappear when we read the Quran and will teach it to our children until the Day of Resurrection?" The Prophet said:

ثَكِلَتْكَ أُمُّكَ زِيَادُ إِنْ كُنْتُ لَأَرَاكَ مِنْ أَفْقَهِ رَجُلٍ بِالْمَدِينَةِ أَوَلَيْسَ هَذِهِ الْيَهُودُ وَالنَّصَارَى يَقْرَءُونَ التَّوْرَاةَ وَالْإِنْجِيلَ لَا يَعْمَلُونَ بِشَيْءٍ مِمَّا فِيهِمَا

May your mother be bereft of you, Ziyad! I thought you were the wisest man in Medina. Do not these Jews and Christians read the Torah and the Gospel, but they do not act upon what is in them?

Jabir reported: The Messenger of Allah, peace and blessings be upon him, said:

إِنَّمَا شِفَاءُ الْعِيِّ السُّؤَالُ

Verily, the only cure for ignorance is to ask questions.

Ibn al-Qayyim commented on this tradition, writing:

وَقَدْ جَعَلَ النَّبِيُّ صَلَّى اللَّهُ عَلَيْهِ وَسَلَّمَ الْجَهْلَ دَاءً وَجَعَلَ دَوَاءَهُ سُؤَالَ الْعُلَمَاءِ

The Prophet (s) designated ignorance as a disease and he designated the cure as asking the scholars.

Hadith 34

Abdullah ibn Amr reported: The Messenger of Allah, peace and blessings be upon him, said:

مَنْ تَطَبَّبَ وَلَمْ يُعْلَمْ مِنْهُ طِبٌّ قَبْلَ ذَلِكَ فَهُوَ ضَامِنٌ

Whoever practices medicine without any prior knowledge of medicine will be held liable.

Hadith 35

Zayd ibn Arqam reported: The Messenger of Allah, peace and blessings be upon him, said:

اللَّهُمَّ إِنِّي أَعُوذُ بِكَ مِنْ عِلْمٍ لاَ يَنْفَعُ وَمِنْ قَلْبٍ لاَ يَخْشَعُ وَمِنْ نَفْسٍ لاَ تَشْبَعُ وَمِنْ دَعْوَةٍ لاَ يُسْتَجَابُ لَهَا

O Allah, I seek refuge in you from knowledge that does not benefit, from a heart that is not reverent, from a soul that is not content, and from a supplication that is not answered.

Hadith 36

Ibn Abbas reported: It was said, "O Messenger of Allah, which gathering is best?" The Prophet, peace and blessings be upon him, said:

مَنْ ذَكَّرَكُمُ اللَّهَ رُؤْيَتُهُ وَزَادَ فِي عِلْمِكُمْ مَنْطِقُهُ وَذَكَّرَكُمْ بِالآخِرَةِ عَمَلُهُ

A gathering of those who inspire you to remember Allah when you see them, whose discourse increases your knowledge, and whose good deeds inspire you to remember the Hereafter.

Hadith 37

Abu Barzah reported: The Messenger of Allah, peace and blessings be upon him, said:

لَا تَزُولُ قَدَمَا عَبْدٍ يَوْمَ الْقِيَامَةِ حَتَّى يُسْأَلَ عَنْ عُمُرِهِ فِيمَا أَفْنَاهُ وَعَنْ عِلْمِهِ فِيمَ فَعَلَ وَعَنْ مَالِهِ مِنْ أَيْنَ اكْتَسَبَهُ وَفِيمَ أَنْفَقَهُ وَعَنْ جِسْمِهِ فِيمَ أَبْلَاهُ

The feet of a servant will not move on the Day of Resurrection until he is asked about his lifetime and how he used it, his knowledge and how he acted upon it, his wealth and from where he acquired it and how he spent it, and his body and how he exhausted it.

Hadith 38

Abu Huraira reported: The Messenger of Allah, peace and blessings be upon him, said:

اللَّهُمَّ انْفَعْنِي بِمَا عَلَّمْتَنِي وَعَلِّمْنِي مَا يَنْفَعُنِي وَزِدْنِي عِلْمًا

O Allah, benefit me with what you have taught me, teach me what will benefit me, and increase my knowledge.

Hadith 39

Jundub ibn Abdullah reported: The Messenger of Allah, peace and blessings be upon him, said:

مَثَلُ الْعَالِمِ الَّذِي يُعَلِّمُ النَّاسَ الْخَيْرَ وَيَنْسَى نَفْسَهُ كَمَثَلِ السِّرَاجِ يُضِيءُ لِلنَّاسِ وَيَحْرِقُ نَفْسَهُ

The parable of the scholar who teaches people virtue but forgets himself, is that of a lamp giving people light while it burns itself.

Hadith 40

Aisha reported: The Messenger of Allah, peace and blessings be upon him, said:

إِنَّ أَبْغَضَ الرِّجَالِ إِلَى اللهِ الأَلَدُّ الْخَصِمُ

Verily, the most hated man to Allah is the one who is 'fiercest in argument.'

The Quran (2:204)

Hadith 41

Abu Huraira reported: The Messenger of Allah, peace and blessings be upon him, said:

مَنْ أُفْتِيَ بِغَيْرِ عِلْمٍ كَانَ إِثْمُهُ عَلَى مَنْ أَفْتَاهُ وَمَنْ أَشَارَ عَلَى أَخِيهِ بِأَمْرٍ يَعْلَمُ أَنَّ الرُّشْدَ فِي غَيْرِهِ فَقَدْ خَانَهُ

Whoever is given an opinion not based on knowledge, his sin falls upon the one who gave him the opinion. Whoever directs his brother to a matter of which he knows good lies elsewhere, he has betrayed him.

Hadith 42

Abu Huraira reported: The Messenger of Allah, peace and blessings be upon him, said:

الْكَلِمَةُ الْحِكْمَةُ ضَالَّةُ الْمُؤْمِنِ فَحَيْثُ وَجَدَهَا فَهُوَ أَحَقُّ بِهَا

The word of wisdom is the lost property of the believer. Wherever he finds it, he is most deserving of it.

The source of the 42 Hadith

HADITH	SOURCE
1	Sunan Ibn Mājah 224, Grade: Sahih
2	Ṣaḥīḥ Muslim 2699, Grade: Sahih
3	Sunan Abī Dāwūd 3641, Grade: Sahih
4	Sunan al-Tirmidhī 2685, Grade: Sahih
5	Ṣaḥīḥ al-Bukhārī 71, Grade: Muttafaqun Alayhi Al-Mu'jam al-Kabīr 929, Grade: Hasan
6	Musnad Aḥmad 9880, Grade: Sahih Jāmi' Bayān al-'Ilm 619
7	Ṣaḥīḥ al-Bukhārī 79, Grade: Muttafaqun Alayhi
8	Ṣaḥīḥ al-Bukhārī 73, Grade: Muttafaqun Alayhi
9	Ṣaḥīḥ al-Bukhārī 4739, Grade: Sahih
10	Ṣaḥīḥ al-Bukhārī 2847, Grade: Muttafaqun Alayhi
11	Ṣaḥīḥ al-Bukhārī 3274, Grade: Sahih
12	Sunan Abī Dāwūd 3663, Grade: Sahih Fatḥ al-Bārī 3274
13	Sunan Abī Dāwūd 3660, Grade: Sahih
14	Ṣaḥīḥ Muslim 2674, Grade: Sahih
15	Sunan al-Tirmidhī 2677, Grade: Hasan
16	Ṣaḥīḥ Muslim 1631, Grade: Sahih Sunan Ibn Mājah 242, Grade: Hasan
17	Sunan al-Tirmidhī 2647, Grade: Sahih
18	Sunan al-Tirmidhī 2686, Grade: Sahih Jāmi' Bayān al-'Ilm 423

HADITH	SOURCE
19	Sunan al-Tirmidhī 2322, Grade: Hasan
20	Ṣaḥīḥ al-Bukhārī 100, Grade: Muttafaqun Alayhi
21	Musnad Aḥmad 8396, Grade: Hasan Al-Muwaṭṭa' 384
22	Al-Muʻjam al-Kabīr 10239, Grade: Sahih
23	Ṣaḥīḥ Ibn Ḥibbān 6352, Grade: Hasan
24	Sunan Ibn Mājah 226, Grade: Sahih
25	Sunan al-Tirmidhī 2654, Grade: Hasan
26	Sunan Abī Dāwūd 3664, Grade: Sahih
27	Sunan al-Tirmidhī 2649, Grade: Sahih
28	Sunan Ibn Mājah 3843, Grade: Hasan
29	Sunan al-Tirmidhī 2950, Grade: Sahih
30	Sunan al-Tirmidhī 2167, Grade: Sahih
31	Al-Ādāb lil-Bayhaqī 818, Grade: Sahih
32	Sunan Ibn Mājah 4048, Grade: Sahih
33	Sunan Abī Dāwūd 336, Grade: Sahih Al-Jawāb al-Kāfī 1/8
34	Sunan Ibn Mājah 3466, Grade: Sahih
35	Ṣaḥīḥ Muslim 2722, Grade: Sahih
36	Musnad Abī Yaʼlá 2408, Grade: Hasan

HADITH	SOURCE
37	Sunan al-Tirmidhī 2417, Grade: Sahih
38	Sunan al-Tirmidhī 3599, Grade: Hasan
39	al-Mu'jam al-Kabīr, Grade: Sahih
40	Ṣaḥīḥ Muslim 2668, Grade: Sahih
41	Sunan Abī Dāwūd 3657, Grade: Hasan
42	Sunan al-Tirmidhī 2687, Grade: Hasan

Success comes from Allah,
and Allah knows best

For more educational books about Islam, please visit our author page: "**Aicha Mhamed**"
You have also found a book that talks about Islamic prayer, Islam history, Ramadan and others.

Made in the USA
Las Vegas, NV
03 December 2023

82012368R00036